Outer-Body Travel

poems by

Kathleen Ellis

Finishing Line Press
Georgetown, Kentucky

Outer-Body Travel

For RW and in memory of Pica,
who traveled widely

ACKNOWLEDGMENTS

Versions of the following poems first appeared in the following publications:

The Café Review: "Black Hole," "Heliopause"
Common Ground Review: "The April Pool," "Morning Ghazal at Lake Merritt"
The Hurricane Review: "Adrift in the Kidney-Shaped Pool"
Red Rock Review: "What the Body Knows"

Publisher: Leah Maines

Editor: Christen Kincaid

Cover Art: Wikipedia Commons, in Public Domain

Author Photo: Photo courtesy of UMaine Marketing and Communication

Cover Design: Elizabeth Maines McCleavy

Printed in the USA on acid-free paper.
Order online: www.finishinglinepress.com
also available on amazon.com

Author inquiries and mail orders:
Finishing Line Press
P. O. Box 1626
Georgetown, Kentucky 40324
U. S. A.

Table of Contents

BLACK HOLES CAN SING

To sing, was singing, the lowest note
in the universe, too low for humans
to hear, 57 octaves below middle C.
Is there a score for the longest note
in the universe?
                         For the human voice
as it strains to listen to the energy
its notes carry and never reach us?

Is there a song in all its voices
whose original has vanished
as sound waves oscillating out
from the B-flat edge

                         of a black hole?
The sound is my breath
escaping the human galaxy.

ADRIFT IN THE KIDNEY-SHAPED POOL

I too am floating.
I take the shape of water,
blue as the origin of countries
on some ever-changing map—

And like light,
body bends in water,

breaking away
from the curvature of earth—
(the toes curled under like an enigma)

It's best to place your legs
apart, even as they move slowly
closer in the shifting blue—

as it is better
to let your arms dangle,
feel the gravity

of the head arching back,
even as somewhere
between hip and waist

the body deepens,
until we wonder which part
of us is floating—

a globe's curving over
into water, it laps
from brown to blue.

BLUE MOON

Once in a blue moon
we meet and tell each other
lies about the world

Once in a blue moon
I open my eyes underwater
and see the moon rising over the river

Moon for the long forgotten
Moonless nights, we go to sleep
with our bodies on

MERCURY RISING
After Sappho

Naughty boy,
Hermes shook my limbs of least resistance.

WHAT THE BODY KNOWS

This morning, driving alone
across the coastal barrens
I know for a moment
how the field waves to itself.

The acres of last year's berries
have erupted into their native ruby,
not the bluish-red of their sweet tartness,
but wine-red, like the daylight

breaking into the body's window,

where like these barrens
the body replicates itself,
cell into cell, tissue and fibers,
the contractions of desire—

Listen, you can hear the body
asking to be released, wanting
to bloom the way fields bloom—
in skin and stones and the ordinary.

LIMBO

Suggesting paired human limbs evolved from a pair of fins,
and before that from fishes' gills,

a German anatomist in 1878 may have been
on the right track.

In his time, Gegenbaur's theory was contentious,
but now we have the Sonic Hedgehog gene

to prove it, and it's okay to assume
our limbs have evolved from shark fins—

Which amounts to what?
That Sonic Hedgehog tells the limb

which side will be the thumb
and which side will be the pinky?

That survival is as convoluted as, say,
a leap of faith, something finny, the body of "facts"

of my mother, a Christian Scientist,
who insisted *there is no truth in matter,*

professing nobody is body.

VENUS ENVY

Her birth is highly suspect. The ultimate cover-up. Blown into being by zephyrs full grown on the half shell. Scallop shell for a vulva. A great ploy of modesty to pretend she doesn't have one. Botticelli liked her thin and pagan, but, others liked her plump. De Milo, De'Medici, Venus Felix, Venus Genetrix. Titian's is unclothed. Scandalous. Big-breasted goddesses and long-legged ones. Armless ones and voluptuous ones. Her shape grew fatter over time. Yet women wish they were her, and men desire her. It is not so easy to abandon the body. Brush her golden locks. Pull her hand away from her belly. Lift her hair and gaze on her slender neck.

STRANGE BRAIN

Brain we must engorge and fill,
all three pounds of convoluted mass.

Brain nearly double the size of other
mammals except the sperm whale.

Brain that thinks and dreams and laughs,
appearing 66 times in Shakespeare's plays.

Drab brain, colored gray and white.
Brain with its 70,000 thoughts each day.

Brain with its hippocampus, which
is not an ancient river horse.

Hard-wired, brain encrypted with ambition.
Brain on jet lag. Brain on dopamine.

Brain whose cavity is stuffed with sage.
Brain that is sixty percent fat.

Brain to be stormed and teased.
Brain that senses a change of heart.

Brain that controls our every excitation.
Brain of the cocky walk, the aimless shuffle.

Brain on anomia, tip-of-the-tongue syndrome.
Brain with its selective memory, curved time.

Brain that speaks its mind, cuts to the quick,
as if it all really matters.

THE EVE HYPOTHESIS

1

If we are lucky,
it will not take three million years
to imagine how the dead might
admire this halo of cities,
but for now we must follow
how one bone leads to another.
As in excavation, dirt flies upward
so allegory takes wing against
wreckage of bones, the shifting sands,
a gully in its narrow channel.

In whose interest do we labor,
whose shadows of desire
cast back at us the orphaned event?
When no woman remembers
her mother (or is it her daughter?),
what can measure our loss—
afarensis as *africanus*?
A beginning, but what begins?

2

Found near Hadar:
Female: a bit of thighbone,
couple of vertebrae, pieces of jaw,
part of a pelvis and some ribs.
A woman keeps coming, hundreds
of bones unearthed in the gully
and pieced together: Adult female,
three feet eight, sixty-five pounds,
three million years; the survivor—

At the vanishing point,
this smallish girl comes down
out of the trees and onto the uplands,
taking the steps she cannot refuse—
the place itself is inconsolable,
its stunted and rain-parched trees,
the hauntingly beautiful names
of Lucy and her cousins—

speaking in hoarse whispers
of what cannot be recovered:
the flesh they long for or dread
the flesh they are sorry to give us
ululating, ululating, lamenting

the thing not exorcised.

3

Face to face: here we are
stripped of our loose skirts.
Look how we resemble you
with our flattened foreheads,
our bones equally dense, the same
drought conditions keeping
no vision but history's—

We see ourselves in you—
somewhat fuller figure, taller,
the same telltale pelvis
flowing between us, proving
you had a bipedal stride—
the unmarked grave,
no headstone, only a small note
out of the ribcage, echoing,
hooting, this ululating.

4

I want five minutes with you
in a cave contemplating your bones
                    maybe five years
in an underground train bound for the surface
an island of light in the heart of a dark continent
the time that takes the place of a lifeline.
Promise you won't hold anything back, you
won't vanish into the back of your oversized brain
that you won't defect to the Kalahari
                    that we'll link hands
like two omnivorous primates
        give up our arboreal life and swagger upright
                knowing we are all Lucy, all wandering
                    in the dark, all Eve, Isis,
                            terrestrial
        brought back to the house we were born in.

5

It's rough for the women who curl up
near a warm grate or in a shelter.
After three million years,
all of us have reached our limit
between the long thighs
of memory.

My body is a memorial.
If I love you, I remember you.
We live only by our relations,
even if we doubt the existence
of the event that is impregnable:
the only variant is your name.

Did some Lucy, some Eve,
have sisters and cousins who
knew the reason for every
fracture in the pelvic girdle?

Tell me their names,
the names of the bones
you love, you lover of bones:
tell me their names, begin
to assemble flesh of my flesh
on these myriad bones.

6

When I press my hips against the X-ray
of your shattered pelvis, we're a perfect fit.
In the bones of my pelvic girdle, the ring
of bones of my girdle, the bones of my
wide-ringed girdle, my wide-rimmed cup
my cavity, my funnel, my water, my basin,
light, light my sacrum, bushy light, in the
exposed sacrum and coccyx, lit round and
round, round inlet in the crevice, in the
wide crevice, in the wide, wide crevice in
the curve, in the bony crevice, in the bony
curve of my old Aunt Lucy, my Lucy,
my Eve, knitting shard into shard, inlet
and outlet, shutting it back up this crack,
this crease, these curves of ilium, of us.

DESERT MUSIC FOR FEMUR & TIBIA
After a drawing by Susan Groce

It turns out the tibia is larger
but the femur is stronger.

Yet in the rarefied air of the desert,
our bones are brittle as tortillas
baked too long in their skins.

Who saw the bones rise in thin air?
Was it a sheep hounded by a hyena?
A woman pursued by a man?

Who saw the shinbone split from the thigh?
Not the desert, blank and deflecting,

where two can't lock together
from pelvis to ankle bone.

Is it too soon—or too late—
to hear the parched breath of the flute?

Hollowed bone, desert music.

BREAKING AND ENTERING

To sense the body   underneath the body
waiting for   the mind to recapitulate

to a purely biological   unfolding of events
to give new form   or expression to

is to suppose   the body   is more than
the changes   in your life   more than

your shadow   or your aura   more than
the light   from behind   your eyes

looking in   and your throat   swelling
as your enter   in this way   breaking out

of your dark interior   singing
I've got you under my skin

MORNING GHAZAL AT LAKE MERRITT

My friend Richard invites me to Tai Chi by the lake.
Unruffled water in the tangerine brushstroke of the lake.

Everyone is Asian but me and the rowers bending.
The festival lights still blinking at dawn around the lake.

l stand in the back row mimicking what I see, Richard
twisting and bowing in the fluid language of the lake.

We see ourselves in the mirror of highrise condos—
their luxury view of our mindless postures by the lake.

I've got black Chinese slippers in my backpack:
the only footwear of resilience beside the lake.

Alone with ourselves, all of us stretching in silence,
the dance of the waist, the curve of the hip of the lake.

There are so many motions, he says, at the edge of skin—
Listen, you can hear your body slow-dance by the lake.

NIGHT SWIMMING
After David Hockney's Midnight Pool (Paper Pool 10)

The midnight pool is like the war, seeing itself
through the infrared of greenish hues.

At night you don't look at the surface at all
and seeing the bodies in the eerie glow,

you also see that the light from within the pool
stops at the surface—

you can see the steps and the rest of it
but the light under the diving board is black,

which is where I lose you
in the space relecting only the faintest light—

You have a thirst for the undrinkable,
the improbable part of what is probable.

You wait between gulps of air, treading the waves
you've generated, letting the dim light absorb you

before the long, protruding shadow,
or maybe your body, flickers—

the water stays dark and cold.

SHADOWS
After David Hockney's The Diver (Paper Pool 18)

Reflection of trees behind the pool
just looking, you could look and look
and all you are doing is looking
at the surface and not into the water.
And depending on the off-again on-again
weather, each day is different—you can
look right through it or onto it or into it.
And while you are still looking at the surface,
the bottom of the pool catches more light
distortion of the figure   under water,
the arms lengthening   the body
going odd and now you can see
the wavy shadow of the diving board
on the bottom, making another shadow—
also distance—the lives you've discarded—
or maybe you think you are one of the trees
bearing traces, any body darkening the water.

AUTUMN POOL

After David Hockney's Autumn Pool (Paper Pool 29)

Seen into, the watery paper of the painted pool
is the rippled light of your childhood, the blue
innuendos in every room you cannot remain in.
It's there in the unquiet ideas that pull and
drag one sidestroke at a time, and those
who do not own a little pool of their own
are contrite and fearful of those who do.
But owning one takes up your life:
It cannot be replaced with a car or lover,
a watchdog or wife, although it can be ignored,
denied, and betrayed, by refusing to skim
off the leaves or vacuum the ones already sinking
to the bottom where they clog up the drain
and remind you of the pleasurable life you were
reluctant to lead, all of them watching you—
the figure that kicks one foot after the other,
and the small leaves, now underwater, congealing.

THE APRIL POOL

A day after the snowmelt and the night before spring
the tarp filled with water
where there had been none.

Water has four acts—
in the last it is disappearing
until the one pool fitting

into other pools, every form
fitting into every other—
bright into dark, sloshing.

And after that,
the water notices the children
with their fingers wrapped around

the holes of the cyclone fence and
the brave, tiniest children dying to enter
the water and kick their legs and paddle.

Could the water have said to the tarp,
I saved you? Could the pool have known
it would survive another winter under cover?

LOLITA

I was reading
Reading Lolita in Tehran
when all of a sudden
you looked up from your book
on Marco Polo and said I looked
like a woman who has just put on the veil.
The cat, scurrying past in her mad dash
to the kitchen, stumbled over
my new invisibility.

HOLDING THE BREATH

Sometimes I swim out to the farthest reaches.
I float with what I was
and with the missing body
on the water of what I am.

And sometimes I swim beneath myself.
Then I hold my breath
in the body of what I'm not.

But there's still another body
in which I'll dive into the center
as though this were the only one there is.

FLYING LEAP

We are "bees of the invisible,"
Rilke tells us.

Another little-known fact:
Water is the only element

that offers more resistance,
the harder you hit it.

Now, I'll tell you a secret:
a child with water wings

climbs to the high-dive platform
from where she takes a flying leap

from the visible to the invisible—
this is the flight of bees

it brings no splash, no ripple.

BLUE CRASH

Every wave works its way toward land.
But not everyone can ride the crest.
I am thirteen and panicking. Disorder
in *the blue crash and the breaking up of*

body as I see it in water, blue
against the slippery white skin—

Ghostly mammal, florid but buoyant.

And salt gets into everything.
Blank and deflecting—
the endless entering into.

TREADING WATER

When I was a girl

I swam out of the body
whose image dives again and again

into the center
of the widest ocean

I made myself weightless
on purpose for this entering into

Blue the first color
And darker still beneath my fins

my legs drifting past me, appearing
and disappearing.

THE FLIMSINESS OF RUMOR

In one version, two men drown in a squall
when their kayaks roll. A woman survives.

In another, no one survives but a rumor spreads
of a man and a woman lost off Petit Manan

and only the guide has survived. Now greater
concern is for man and wife, and we place

our faith in rumor and cross our fingers.
It turns out the guide was married too.

The body count reverses itself.

Two men drown when their kayaks roll
and the two women left are suddenly part

of the same equation. The tide shifts
in spite of itself, revealing again

the changes that bring us to ourselves.
At night the waves rise up like stream.

THE WIDE DISTURBANCES OF WATER

I may never see the earth from space
but when I glance out the window
somewhere over the Gulf
I am hurtling toward the splashdown—

Outside the window, the ghost
of a woman breaking into shapes
mirrors the distance to myself,
as I view the tumultous world

pitching over as we plunge through—

MOON CHART

You take the moon to heart
like Kepler calling it a dream
in his *Somnium*. Flying there,
a human is a force field
protected from intrusions.
The shield goes up, the pressure
mounting like the love you've
dodged or leave behind.
Even the carrot dangling
before your eyes, the craters
growing larger at approach,
suggest impending danger.
The face up close
is pock-marked.
To distract yourself,
you look back and see
the Earth is round.

THE SQUARE-SHOULDERED MAN
SUPPORTING THE HEAVENS

Stunned to learn the man who proved the earth
   is curved from a single photo taken in 1934
      over a South Dakota field was my neighbor,
         Capt. Albert Stevens from Belfast, Maine.
            Rather, he would have been my neighbor
               if I'd been born decades earlier. And
                  in his 1934 flight, the first thing he
                    did after the balloon burst and his
                      gondola plunged to earth was
                        pick himself up off the prairie
                        field and shake off the burden
                        of the heavens. At 72,000 feet
                      space acquires color—blue
                    of dusk acknowledging water,
                 the water, a flatness so expansive
               it seems to gather height, and
            the mountains bordering are
         without shadow—black solidity.
       At this distance, I am what: an eye?
     And this distance? We think we know
   where this is going. How powerful it feels
to play the Titan bearing the burden, spreading
his legs and hoisting the sky upon his shoulders.
How brazenly we curve the world to ourselves.

MR. UNIVERSE

Your vest is a dead giveaway
with its planets and redundant suns
circling your chest.

As you turn, little pieces
of the universe hold forth
for an instant and disappear.

They say the universe is expanding,
but there are parts where
nothing is happening.

Not far from us
the Andromeda Galaxy
is drifting toward the Milky Way.

When I saw the ancient charts
of Earth at the orbital center
of the cosmos, I felt the Earth

stand still, or was *I* standing still,
attracted to nothing but myself?
Is this how it is outside this world?

I am solid, stable, and unmoving.
I am completely at rest,
geocentric.

As children, we were cautioned
to stay put, not move a muscle.
So much obedience leads to inertia.

We hold our breath:
To shift the paradigm, rotate
the man with the universe vest.

DON'T TOUCH, DON'T STARE

Dear Neil:
Heaven forbid I would begrudge
your easy access to the stars.
The biggest star I've ever met
was John Wayne whose toupee
flew off and over my head from
his yacht in Catalina Harbor.
He was relishing success, and
I was hallooing him from the
dock to glimmer in his aura.
Sad, my lack of humility—
At a certain distance, stars are
meant to be gazed upon, even
ours on the outskirts of the galaxy.

BLUE MARBLE

Photo from Apollo 17, the last manned lunar mission, 1972

Out there,
astronauts reach out to fondle you.
In this pulling away from earth,
what we expect is the unexpected.
Irrational lives on a spreadsheet
orbiting the chest, where we cross
our hearts and hope to live another
day, a month, a year or eighty.
Whatever we said, we didn't mean it.
Our intentions go beyond the object of desire—
that blue marble we see as ours, as us.

Excuses, excuses. Alibis stand on their own
recognizance. The more distant the object,
the bluer it seems. So said Leonardo.
A short line of sight through air seems transparent.
Like glass. Like us. It is easy to see
the large island off the coast of Africa.
How did it get that strange name?
How do we know anything?

Think how this would lead to thinking
about the heart's own smart
camera, as if changing focus
could resurrect the old stories, how
gazing at the moon could save the world.
That there are objects called marbles is a fact.

BLACK MARBLE

Photo from Apollo 17, the last manned lunar mission, 1972

At eleven, I signed up to go to the moon
at the Academy of Sciences in Golden Gate Park.
The boy next to me nudged my shoulder,
said, *You know it's black in space.*

As we passed from the Foucault pendulum
into the planetarium,
the lights were already dimming
until it was pitch black.

In the dark, I thought and thought
about the alligators in their concrete pit,
as if a darkness from below might be drawn

into the edge of a bottomless continuum.
As if this might shake us by the teeth
back into the Paleocene.

OUTER-BODY TRAVEL

In the space between us

the body forgets its earthly self.

After two months in flight,

calluses on the bottoms of our feet
    molt and fall off
        softening
        from lack of use

Without gravity, what is the use of muscles
we no longer need for standing up?

And what is the use of tears
we cannot shed while crying?

We leave the world and feel a world
where we're no longer walking upright.

The journey slowly decomposes
the ball of the foot, then the arch
the instep and the heel,

and, not without regret, the sole.

HELIOPAUSE

In this place where the wind
from the sun gives way to the wind
from the stars
the Earth waits for its guests
to return to her
to lie on her sandy beaches
to summit her peaks
to speak her 6,900 languages
to master just one
to make up for lost time
to beg the question
to accept the kindness of strangers
recalling the few times
you have paused
before you leaped through air,
knowing whatever
boundaries you push, you are drawn
back to the breath you live in.